NATIVE AMERICAN
RECIPES >>>>>>>>>>>>>>>>>>>>>>>>>

By Leslie Beckett

KidHaven
PUBLISHING

Published in 2017 by
KidHaven Publishing, an Imprint of Greenhaven Publishing, LLC
353 3rd Avenue
Suite 255
New York, NY 10010

Designer: Andrea Davison-Bartolotta
Editor: Jennifer Lombardo

Photo credits: Cover (bottom) DeAgostini/Getty Images; cover (top) Komngui/Shutterstock.com; back cover, pp. 2, 3, 9, 13, 17, 19, 21–24 (wood texture) Maya Kruchankova/Shutterstock.com; p. 5 MelvinDyson/Shutterstock.com; p. 7 Joseph Sohm/Shutterstock.com; pp. 8, 19 (zucchini) Bihn Thanh Bui/Shutterstock.com; pp. 9, 13, 17, 19, 21 (notebook) BrAt82/Shutterstock.com; p. 9 (inset) Dream79/Shutterstock.com; p. 11 (inset) LeshaBu/Shutterstock.com; p. 11 (main) Sekar B/Shutterstock.com; p. 12 Victor Maschek/Shutterstock.com; p. 13 (inset) Yulia-Bogdanova/Shutterstock.com; p. 14 robert cicchetti/Shutterstock.com; p. 15 Alis Photo/Shutterstock.com; p. 16 Heike Rau/Shutterstock.com; p. 17 (inset) Jeff Wasserman/Shutterstock.com; p. 19 (green pepper) Mr.Nakorn/Shutterstock.com; p. 19 (corn) Neamov/Shutterstock.com; p. 19 (sunflower seeds) draconus/Shutterstock.com; p. 21 (cup) Africa Studio/Shutterstock.com.

Cataloging-in-Publication Data

Names: Beckett, Leslie.
Title: Native American recipes / Leslie Beckett.
Description: New York : KidHaven Publishing, 2017. | Series: Cooking your way through American history | Includes index.
Identifiers: ISBN 9781534520929 (pbk.) | ISBN 9781534520936 (6 pack) ISBN 9781534520943 (library bound) | ISBN 9781534520950 (E-book)
Subjects: LCSH: Indians of North America–Food–Juvenile literature. | Indian cooking–North America–Juvenile literature.

Classification: LCC E98.F7 B43 2017 | DDC 641.597–dc23

Printed in the United States of America

CPSIA compliance information: Batch #CW17KL: For further information contact Greenhaven Publishing LLC, New York, New York at 1-844-317-7404.

Please visit our website, www.greenhavenpublishing.com. For a free color catalog of all our high-quality books, call toll free 1-844-317-7404 or fax 1-844-317-7405.

CONTENTS

TRADITIONAL NATIVE AMERICAN FOODS

Native Americans living in the United States today eat very different foods than they did before the **settlers** arrived. Julie, a nine-year-old girl who lived on a Navajo **reservation** in Arizona, ate hamburgers, pancakes, ice cream, and other foods, just like everyone else. However, sometimes she still ate **traditional** Navajo foods. Fry bread was her favorite. This made her wonder about other traditional Native American foods that she had never tried before.

Different groups of Native Americans lived across what's now the United States, so they had different kinds of foods depending on what was available. Groups that lived near the ocean, for example, used a lot of fish in their cooking. Some groups lived in the desert, some lived in the forest, and some lived on the **plains**. Julie and her family decided to go on a road trip and talk to other Native Americans about the traditional foods in their areas.

The foods Native Americans ate in the past were different than the ones they eat today.

SOME THINGS IN COMMON

Julie learned that even though different groups ate different foods, some things were the same for almost all early Native Americans. All Native Americans ate the plants, berries, fruits, and vegetables that grew on their homelands. Some grew their own food. Others gathered these foods from the land. Most Native Americans hunted for meat, too. Nearly all Native American people grew corn. Corn was considered very important, or **sacred**. People who lived where corn wouldn't grow traded things such as meat or furs with groups that did grow it.

Julie learned that the five major areas where Native Americans lived in what is now the United States were the Southwest, the Pacific Coast, the Great Plains, the Northeast, and the South. The food each group made depended on the plants and animals in each area.

Some Native American groups still hold dances to **celebrate** how important corn is to them.

HOPI, ZUNI, AND PUEBLO

Southwestern groups such as the Hopi, Zuni, and Pueblo lived in the desert, where not much food grows. Julie learned that they grew crops such as corn, beans, squash, and melons. They also hunted rabbits and antelope, and they gathered wild plants such as yucca fruits and potatoes. Because food was sometimes hard to grow or find, it was highly respected by these groups.

To prepare for times when the crops wouldn't grow, groups in the Southwest stored food such as corn and beans. When they couldn't find other food, they would eat cactus fruits and **currants**. These groups, like most Native Americans, would share their food with each other because they believed no food should go to waste or be eaten alone.

yucca

fry bread

Ingredients:

2 cups flour
1 teaspoon baking powder
½ teaspoon salt
warm water
¼ cup vegetable oil

Directions:

- Sift together the flour, baking powder, and salt into a bowl.
- Slowly add warm water while stirring. Keep adding water until you have dough that feels like mud.
- Mix and **knead** the dough with your hands until it's smooth. If the dough is sticky, sprinkle with flour.
- Cover the dough with a towel, and let it rest for 10 minutes.
- Break the dough into pieces the size of a lemon. Roll each piece into a ball, and flatten into a pancake.
- Heat the oil in a heavy frying pan. Add as many pieces of bread as will fit in the pan.
- Fry the pieces of bread on each side until they're brown.
- Take the brown fry bread out of the oil, and place them on a plate covered with a paper towel.
- Serve the fry bread with salt or maple syrup.

This serves about four people.

KWAKIUTL, SKOKOMISH, AND QUILEUTE

The Kwakiutl, Skokomish, and Quileute were a few of the groups that lived in the Pacific Coast area of present-day Canada and the United States. Many plants grow there, including berries, nuts, and mushrooms. It's near the ocean and many rivers, so Native Americans could catch fish, mussels, clams, and sometimes even seals and whales. There were also many wild animals in the forests that they could hunt.

Julie found out that the Pacific Coast groups cooked their fish over hot coals, as many people do today on a barbeque grill. They steamed **shellfish** on heated rocks. When they caught more fish than they could eat, they smoked it to keep it from spoiling so they could eat it throughout the winter. They would also catch otters and seals so they could trade the furs with other Native Americans.

Salmon was an important fish to the Pacific Coast tribes, so they often drew pictures of it.

SIOUX, ARAPAHO, AND CROW

On her trip, Julie discovered that the Native Americans who lived on the plains in the middle of what's now the United States mainly hunted bison for food. They had to follow the bison whenever the animals moved, so the groups couldn't stay in one place long enough to grow many crops. Instead, they gathered plants such as wild rice, fruits, and seeds. They killed only as many bison as they could use. They ate the meat and used the **hides** for clothing and shelter.

When it was hard to find bison, the Native Americans who lived on the plains hunted deer and rabbits. Many groups, such as the Sioux, Arapaho, and Crow, moved with the bison. Others, such as the Mandan, settled in one area and farmed the land. Their crops included corn, pumpkins, squash, and beans.

bison

pumpkin-corn sauce

Ingredients:

1 15-ounce can plain pumpkin (without spices)
1 cup canned or frozen corn
½ teaspoon salt
2 tablespoons honey
vegetable oil

Directions:

- Preheat the oven to 350° Fahrenheit (F). Grease a baking sheet with a small amount of oil.
- Put the corn on the oiled baking sheet, and bake for 20 minutes.
- Mix the corn, pumpkin, salt, and honey in a medium-size pot.
- Heat it over medium heat until it starts to bubble.
- Turn the heat to low, and cook for 10 minutes, stirring from time to time.
- Serve with grilled chicken or pork.

This serves about four people.

Remember to always ask an adult for help when cooking.

HAUDENOSAUNEE, MOHICAN, AND ALGONQUIN

In the northeastern area of what's now the United States, there were forests full of animals and plants for early Native Americans to eat. The Haudenosaunee (Iroquois), Mohican, Algonquin, and other groups hunted elk, moose, and beavers, and they gathered wild berries and fruits. The groups that lived close to the ocean ate fish and shellfish. Some of them tapped maple trees for sap, which could be made into maple syrup.

Many Native Americans who lived in the Northeast were excellent farmers. They grew crops such as corn, beans, pumpkins, and squash. They knew it was important to **fertilize** the soil. Because of this, they were able to farm on the same area of land for many years.

moose

Some Northeastern tribes tapped maple trees and boiled the sap in a log to make maple syrup and maple sugar.

SEMINOLE, CHEROKEE, AND CHICKASAW

Julie discovered the weather in the southern United States is generally very warm. This makes it easy for crops to grow. Native American groups in in the South, such as the Seminole, Cherokee, and Chickasaw, grew corn, sweet potatoes, peanuts, beans, and other crops. Hickory nuts were an important food. Many Native Americans boiled the nuts, squeezed the oil from them, and made a kind of milk that could be used in cooking. They also dried the nuts and ground them into nut flour, which was used to thicken soups and make bread.

The Native Americans in the South also ate meat and fish. They cooked them in thick stews. They also made sweet breads for dessert. Often, they used molasses instead of sugar to make their food sweet.

hickory nuts

baked sweet potato

Ingredients:
4 medium-size sweet potatoes

Directions:
- Preheat the oven to 400° F.
- Scrub the sweet potatoes well under water. Poke them several times with a fork.
- Cover a small baking sheet with aluminum foil. Put the sweet potatoes on the foil, and put the pan in the oven.
- Bake the sweet potatoes for one hour.
- Take the sweet potatoes out of the oven. Serve with butter, brown sugar, or maple syrup.

This serves four people.

Many Native Americans ate sweet potatoes. They cooked them in many different ways, including baking them.

WAYS TO COOK

The early Native Americans didn't have stoves and ovens inside their houses. Instead, they would often roast their meat over an open fire. This fire could be either indoors or outdoors. The Southwestern and Southern groups of Native Americans liked stews, which they cooked in clay pots. The women also baked meat and vegetables in baskets that were covered with clay on the inside. The food and some hot stones would be put into the basket, and the heat from the stones would cook the food.

Some groups would also bury a clay pot under hot coals and uncover it after a few hours. In the Southwest, many groups built large beehive-shaped clay ovens called *hornos*. They would grind corn into a powder using rocks and mix the powder with water and oil. They used the *horno* to bake this into cornbread.

vegetable mush

Ingredients:
2 cups canned corn
1 medium-size zucchini, chopped
1 green pepper, chopped
2 tablespoons sunflower seeds
½ teaspoon salt
½ cup water

Instead of using a blender, Native American women would mash their vegetables between two rocks.

Directions:
- Put all the ingredients into a blender or food processor.
- Add ½ cup of water.
- Turn the machine on and off until it cuts the vegetables into tiny pieces and then mashes them. You may need to add a little more water to help the machine with the mashing.
- Pour the vegetable mixture into a pot, and heat over medium heat. Stir every once in a while.
- When the mixture starts to bubble, turn the heat down low, and cook for 10 minutes.
- Stir often.

This serves two people.

MEALS FOR TRIPS

Early Native Americans didn't have coolers for their food or restaurants to eat at when they traveled. On long trips to hunt bison or catch fish, they would take special foods that were **nutritious**, easy to carry, and didn't spoil quickly.

One such food was called pemmican, or dried meat cakes. Another was jerky, which many people still eat today. Native American jerky was generally made from bison or deer meat, but today's jerky is often made from beef or turkey. People also often carried dried berries or turnips.

On her trip, Julie learned that the animals the Native Americans hunted were sacred to them, so they used every part and thanked the spirit of the animal for helping them **survive**. They would eat the meat, use the hides to make clothing, and use the bones to make weapons or jewelry. Today, Americans waste a lot of food, unlike the early Native Americans.

pinole

Ingredients:
½ cup yellow cornmeal
2 tablespoons honey
½ teaspoon cinnamon
1 cup boiling water

Directions:
- Heat a heavy frying pan on medium-high heat.
- When the pan is hot, sprinkle in the cornmeal to dry roast it.
- Stir until you see the cornmeal starting to turn brown. This will take about six to eight minutes. Keep stirring the cornmeal or it will burn.
- When it's brown, scrape the cornmeal into a small bowl. Mix in honey and cinnamon.
- Stir 1 tablespoon of this mix into one cup of boiling water and let sit for 10 minutes.

This serves one person.

This hot corn drink is nice on cool fall days.

GLOSSARY

celebrate: To honor something important.

currants: Small dried fruits that are like raisins.

fertilize: To make soil rich for growing many crops.

hide: The skin of an animal.

knead: To prepare dough by mixing it with your hands.

nutritious: Containing anything that a living thing needs for energy, to grow, or to heal.

plain: A large, flat piece of land.

reservation: Area of land that is set aside by the government for Native Americans to live on.

sacred: Highly respected, often for religious reasons.

settler: A person who moves to a new land to live.

shellfish: An animal, such as a crab or an oyster, that has a hard outer shell and lives in water.

survive: To keep living.

traditional: Having to do with the ways of doing things in a culture that are passed down from parents to children.

FOR MORE INFORMATION

WEBSITES

Indian Country Diaries

www.pbs.org/indiancountry/index.html
Read about the ways Native Americans are keeping their culture alive today and the problems they have faced throughout history.

Native American Food

www.native-languages.org/food.htm
Learn about how Native Americans' diets changed depending on where they lived, and find extra recipes.

Native American Recipes

www.food.com/topic/native-american/popular
Find more recipes for foods such as fry bread and pumpkin cake.

BOOKS

Connors, Kathleen. *The First Thanksgiving*. New York, NY: Gareth Stevens Publishing, 2014.

Gagne, Tammy. *Life on the Reservations*. Hockessin, DE: Mitchell Lane Publishers, 2014.

Nolan, Frederick W. *Native Peoples*. London, UK: Arcturus Publishing, 2015.

INDEX